"With these poems Jim invites you into his life, touches your heart with the intimate and mends meaning into the mundane."
—Bill Pelz

Opening Jim Carillon's book of poetry, *This Virgin Page*, is like opening the front door to a good childhood friend. After many years as a seeker, here is a man at peace. Right away you want to know his story. These poems are his story: filled with both questions and answers. They tell the reader: I am complete.
—Mamie Davis Hilliard
Author, *And to See Takes Time*

"These accessible, conversational poems are a revealing and unabashed journey—an everyman's journey—through the author's life. Along the way, we savor interludes of simple joys amidst the dilemmas and injustices of life, told with an innocence that leaves both writer and reader vulnerable. The author reminds us that the quest to find or mold an existence that is simultaneously noble and comfortable is as important as it is unattainable."
—Nelson Sartoris
Author, *Brain Slivers, On Wings of Words,* and *With These Hands*

ArsPoetica is an imprint of Pisgah Press, established in 2011 to publish and promote works of quality offering original ideas and insight into the human condition and the world around us.

Copyright © 2020 Jim Carillon

Printed in the United States of America

Published by Pisgah Press, LLC
PO Box 9663, Asheville, NC 28815
www.pisgahpress.com

Cover design & layout by A. D. Reed

All rights reserved. No part of this publication may be reproduced, stored in a retrieval system, or transmitted, in any form or by any means, electronic, mechanical, photocopying, recording, or otherwise, without the prior written permission of Pisgah Press, except in the case of quotations in critical articles or reviews.

Library of Congress Cataloging-in-Publication Data
Carillon, Jim
This Virgin Page
Library of Congress Control Number: 2020923765

ISBN: 978-1-942016595
Poetry/General

First Edition
December 2020

This Virgin Page

Poems

Jim Carillon

Acknowledgments

I first would like to thank all my beloved family members, especially my wife Aline and my recently departed father, Bill Carillon, for being who they are/were and emotionally supporting this work. Thanks also to various members of our local poetry groups who meet regularly to share our writings, provide feedback, and support each other as we write. These include beloved friends from the poetry group at our Unitarian Universalist Congregation of the Swannanoa Valley and two separate Poetry Lovers' groups at the Osher Lifelong Learning Institute at UNC Asheville. Our Fairview Foragers, who hike together each week, also inspire me in countless ways. Finally a big thank you also to my friend Andy Reed, editor of Pisgah Press, who helped to bring these poems to a wider audience.

Contents

Friends and Places I Have Loved

The Cinque Terra 4
Susan 5
Bumps in the Road 6
The Root Cause Farm 7
Volunteering at the Garden in Fall 8
Recipe for Blueberry Picking 9
P. S. Oh How I Love You 10
Living in the Now 12
At the Seward Café 13
Rain, Rain Go Away 14
Record Snowfall 15
Shady Hollow Lodge in Sand Run Park 16
Walden Pond 18
Above the Glacier 19
Thinking of You My Daughter 20

Family

The Kids Are All Right 22
Looking Forward 23
Three Long Days Visit 24
Measures 25
Horizonless View 26
Haiku for You 27
From One Man to One Woman 28
Living with it 30
Between the Sheets 31
In Venice 32
Preventative Maintenance 33
Will He? 34
Thirty Years 36
Gratitude 37
Along Mogadore Road 38
Thanks Dad 39

Contents

Holding Cell Visit 40
Farewell Father 41
Sudden Departure 42
Startling Image 43
Guiding Light in Absentia 44
Graduation Day 45
Angels Landing 46
Your Favorite Song 47
Family Portrait 48

Exercising Body and Mind

Cool Wheels! Announcing the Dual-Sport Hybrid 52
The Second Summit 53
Fortunate Fairview Foragers 54
Making My Own Breezes 56
Cloudy Days 58
Not Waiting 59
35-km Ride to Lake Bolsena 60
This Time Just for Me 61
Against the Wind 62
What Will It Take? 64
Removing Thistles 65

Introspection

Introspection 68
Twenty-Five or Six Past Four 69
Observed Limits to Personal Control 70
Today I Am 72
How to Avoid Becoming Comfortably Numb 73
Worthy Someday? 74
Overcast Day 75
Worn Identities 76
Burnout or a New Happiness? 78
Wish Me Luck 79
Be Here Now 80
Absence 81

Contents

How Do I? 82
Personal Ad 83

Social Justice?
Not-So-Empty Buckets 86
If I Were King 88
White Privilege 90
Reno Baby! 91
Building a Safer World 92
The Leaders We Deserve 93
Weathering the Storm 94
Insignificance 95
Maladapting to Covid-19 96
During This Storm 98
Corona Days 99
Identity 100

Fynnley!
Expecting Again after So Many Years 102
Fostering 103
Welcome Home Fynnley! 104
1:00 a.m. Feeding 105
Worries and Their Antidotes 106
Getting Ready 107
Sleeping Together 108
Balancing Act 109
Dear Mommy 110
Foster Parenting 112
New Best Friends 113
At Five Months 114
Domesticated 115
Early Christmas Gift 116
Reason #847 for Fostering Our Infant Son 118
Happy First Birthday 119
Morning Strolls with Our Foster Son 120
To Our Son 121

Contents

Foster Leaving Time 122
Loved and Lost Again 123
Quiet Morning Stroll 124
Missing You Already 126

Writing

This Virgin Page 128
Sweet Nectarine 129
My Charge 130
After All 131
too many words 132
Managing Stress 133
Some Days Are Like That 134
Dear Aja Monet 135
Only Ten Lines? 136
This White Page 137

About the Author 139

THIS VIRGIN PAGE

POEMS

Friends and Places I Have Loved

THE CINQUE TERRA

From halfway up this hill, our porch provides
A stunning view of the village of Montorosso below.
The quiet of this early pre-dawn moment
Allows me to hear the gently rolling waves on the beach.

The colorful buildings throughout this village,
Many with their red tile roofs, splash warmth
Against the green hills, grape arbors and rugged cliffs
That envelope this now sleeping seaside town.

While seemingly not a soul can be heard nor seen,
A local train breaks the soft sound of the waves
But only for a brief moment or two;
A seagull announces the brightening sky.

Puffy clouds—or is it fog?—crest the hills across the bay
While nearby leaves flutter gently in the cool breeze.
It is these quiet mornings here on this porch
That I'll treasure most about these five lands.

Susan

With more than kindness,
more than compassion,
she plants hardy seeds of
community everywhere and
within everyone she touches.

She shows us the magic is in the soil—
which she tenderly cultivates
with her warm smile,
easy laughter and
meaningful conversations.

Each of us who puts our own hands
in the earth next to her grows
straighter, stronger, so much taller
as we too grow in beauty alongside
the healthy vegetables we grow for others.

She quietly models how to
work with, not for, each other,
harvesting a little grace for ourselves
as we meet the most basic needs
of our neighbors and in each other.

A gentle teacher of all generations in many ways
she is more than a master gardener,
she is the embodiment of Mother Nature herself.
I am simply humbled and honored
to call her my dear friend.

BUMPS IN THE ROAD

My arms feel heavy this morning after last night's
Two hours of loading, hauling, and dumping mulch chips.
Wheelbarrowing a five-and-a-half-year-old back up to
The mulch pile was well worth the extra weight.

We both had even more fun wheelbarrowing her down to
A distant garden spot, she atop the full barrow of mulch,
Especially when we rolled through a pothole or two
Bouncing and her giggling at these bumps in the road.

Community gardening is often like that—
Sometimes unexpected bumps in the road
Never seem quite as bad as we might have feared.
Maybe the rest our lives should be like that too.

Yet as we forked and bumped, rolled and dumped the mulch
In this garden feeding our neighbors in greater need,
I still felt something was missing in all this garden beauty—
Where were even more of our neighbors who were not there?

Those absent last night were missing so much fun:
Of witnessing how beautifully this glorious garden grows,
Of sweating together for neighbors whom we have not yet met,
Of sharing our deeper selves, our very lives as we toil together,

And especially the joy of bouncing with a youngster
Through the inevitable bumps in the road.

The Root Cause Farm

Our community garden is a wonderous place where we
Turn compost and soils into sharing organic foods,
Turn loneliness and lost souls into deep friendships,
Turn new faces and old veterans into helpful neighbors.

Where we invite tears of joy or sorrow along with the rain,
Where we grow children and youth into caring adult citizens,
Where we develop interns into ambassadors for peace,
Where we turn donors and volunteers into community leaders.

Where we share our lives as we share pot-luck dinners,
Where we spread caring along with the compost and mulch,
Where we pull each other up as together we pull weeds,
Where we enrich our relationships as we enrich the soil.

Where we turn givers and receivers into caring neighbors,
Where we support each other as we support climbing plants,
Where we work not for but with each other growing fruits,
Where we grow community as well as healthy vegetables.

Where we welcome everyone along with all the pollinators,
Where handshakes and hugs turn blossoms into harvests,
Where we feed those in need with healthy food and caring,
Where flowers and community together organically bloom.

Care to join this adventure of growing community for all?

Jim Carillon

Volunteering at the Garden in Fall

Interns had cut and stacked some long green stalks,
Laying them in a large pile near the tool shed.
My task tonight to cut and wheelbarrow them
To a new composting row near some still thriving okra.

I start this all too sedentary task in earnest, hoping
To soon move to heavier chores involved with others.
Most of these longer plants are unknown to me except for
A few heavy-headed sunflowers with their thicker stalks.

Maybe I will find a few seeds to take home to
The birdfeeder outside the window by my wife's desk.
Although fringed in their familiar bright yellow petals,
The sunflowers are now barren, their seeds long gone.

The many other plants in this pile were less familiar.
Easier to cut as they narrow to finer and finer branches
With bright red berries fruiting these equally tall stalks—
So unlike other vegetable plants I have previously composted.

Then suddenly—a late blooming flower not yet gone to seed:
Purple, variegated, infinitely more interesting and complex than
The sunflowers, hewn before it could produce its offspring—
Glorious In its delicate beauty before this busy helper.

Pausing while admiring this lovely flower, I began to wonder:
When I too am soon cut down, my financial seeds long dispersed,
Will I leave only sturdy reliable stalks for composting
Or also one last surprise for another gardener to enjoy?

RECIPE FOR BLUEBERRY PICKING

Take an empty gallon jug. Cut the top out (keeping the handle).
Find a patch of wild blueberries or inexpensive pick-your-own farm.
Tie a string through the handle then drape the jug about chest high.
Start picking early to avoid the heat of the August sun.

Wade right into the blueberry bush for the shade and so
You can reach high to grab two or three ripe berries at a time.
Curl them among your fingers, for gentle is always better for everything.
Then gently drop handfuls into your berry bucket on your chest.

Go with a friend or three to listen as you pick, leap-frogging them
Around the bushes, giving each room to reach, pluck and think.
An hour is about as much as you can take in the summer sun,
But you can each fill a gallon if the bushes are full and the berries ripe.

Avoid red ones—"When they're red, they're green," my father used to say.
Choose dusky dark-blue ones of any size as small berries often pack a punch.
Bring your treasure home, spreading berries on a cookie sheet, then into a freezer.
After your berries freeze solid then store them in bags back in the freezer.

But do save a pint of fresh berries, add two ripe peaches and bake them in a pie.
Share the warm pie with your picking friends or other loved ones.
Tell these latter folks how pie is always better with fresh berries,
Enticing them to join you next time you go berry picking.

P.S. Oh, How I Love You
(An homage to the varied lyrics of Paul Simon)

It's a still-life watercolor of a now late afternoon,
I keep listening to some records as my thoughts return to you.
Voices leaking from a sad café, I saw a shadow touch a shadow's hand,
And the song I was writing is left undone.

Last night I had the strangest dream
People writing songs that voices never share, yet
I heard cathedral bells tripping down the alley ways,
And the moon rose over an open field.

I watch as her breasts gently rise, gently fall,
I heard a church bell softly chime in a melody sustaining.
Let the morning time drop all its petals on me,
Michigan seems like a dream to me now.

What a dream I had, softer than the rain:
It was ... a time of innocence, a time of confidences.
I only kiss your shadow, I cannot feel your hand,
You're a stranger now unto me.

Can you imagine us years from today, sharing a park bench quietly?
And when evening falls I will comfort you.
Because a vision softly creeping left its seeds while I was sleeping
But when I come back to bed someone's taken my place.

All lies and jest, still a man hears what he wants to hear and disregards the rest.
Hidden deep within his pocket, he holds a colored crayon.
Blinded by the light of God and truth and right...
But my words come back to me in shades of mediocrity like emptiness in harmony.

Remember me to one who lives there
With words that tear and strain to rhyme.
Half of the time we're gone but we don't know where;
We've all come to look for America!

Living in the Now

This very moment I am so drawn to you,
Not sure what I might next do or say.
Is our deep connection obvious to you as well
Or is this just another unrequited moment?

No matter. I will just take you in,
Breathe in your essence, your beauty.
I shall admire you from across this room
Quietly, cunningly, secretly for now.

I watch as you move, as you think
Wondering what we might have become
In another time, another place, other age perhaps,
When all that keeps me from you were gone.

How ironic: This goal-directed man of action,
This mover and shaker, he who gets it done,
Simply sits here passively—yet fully content—
To just be near you, wondering to himself.

May this very moment last forever and a day.

AT THE SEWARD CAFÉ

An authentic liberal vibe prevails from the
Black Lives Matter sign in the doorway
To the casual staff attire, unusual artwork, and
Slow paced regulars paying more for good food.

Well-worn wooden windows, floors, tables and booths—
The large corner booth filled this morning with businessmen.
Other patrons are mostly couples speaking quietly—
She mostly smiling, he striving too hard to charm.

Exuding a knowing sensuality, is she really
As beautiful as she looks or just so very young?
Either way, she's mesmerizing because they're
Both out of audible reach two booths to the side.

Likely it is not that they're both so very young
But rather that I'm so old and eating alone,
Trying to breathe it all in while savoring my fresh over-easy
Eggs, hash-browns and non-vegan sausage at the Seward Café.

Rain, Rain Go Away

Will this incessant rain ever stop?
Nineteen inches in two weeks with more forecast—
Too much for this mountain community anyways.
Beginning to feel a little moldy myself.

Flooding, power outages, and worst of all
Two lives lost when a tree fell on their car.
Many displaced from their homes and I wonder
How many others affected severely by this rain?

Some rain is better than the last two years
Of heavy drought but enough already!
Makes outdoor events more than challenging
Or commuting by bike nearly impossible.

As in life, a little moderation is in order.
Go away and come again another day
Or week or a month would be soon enough,
Please!

Record Snowfall

Just came in from attempting and failing
to make a dent in removing the snow
from our long steep driveway
after two tries—just now and earlier.

It is still quite a journey of wet snow
between me and yesterday's mail.
So be it. No, so it must be—
My back and breath need to recover.

Absolute proof that I am no longer
the younger man I keep thinking
I am; or likely never was.
Humbled and heavy as this snow with regret.

A half mile and almost 200 feet in elevation:
how hard can it be to cut a single shoveled path
from the garage to the mailbox below?
More than I imagined, more than I can do.

Yet the snow showers have finally eased,
the sun behind the clouds is warming, and
we still have power at least for the moment.
Time now to rest before the next attempt,

And try to take this effort less personally.

Shady Hollow Lodge in Sand Run Park

The hunter's cabin in the park near our parents' homes
Was large enough only for a stone fireplace and
A couple of picnic tables with dim light and many shadows
From two oil lamps hanging from the ceiling.

We met there as we formed our teen group,
The Walden Club, to hike the trails,
Explore the park and each other as we
Shared our favorite quotes from Thoreau.

When we went off to our various colleges and lives
We faithfully returned to rent this old cabin in the park
Each Friday after Thanksgiving, hiking and sharing
Leftovers from our family meals and current lives.

Two couples from this group became two early marriages
But neither lasted—partners too young to really know better.
Now nearly fifty years on I remember those gatherings
With a warmth like the hut's glowing fire after a cold hike.

We nearly were snowed in the last year we met there
Trees cracking under the weight of a heavy wet snow.
Worse fates could befall us we told each other then,
Waiting it out until the ranger forced us to leave.

I'm told the hunter's cabin was replaced with a larger building,
Electrified and plumbed which I consider a loss of its charm.
Our once-steadfast group grew further and further apart,
Each of us blown across the continent these many years since.

Looking it up today on the internet I find ironically that
The modern replacement cabin burned down last year,
With construction of an even larger cabin now underway.
The new air-conditioned cabin will be available for rent next year.

But I will choose not to return hundreds of miles to rent this cabin
Still accessible by car near the ford beyond its hidden entrance.
Rather, I shall hold the original old hunter's cabin as a fond memory
Of those forever fast friends and a much simpler time and place.

Some places and times should only be accessed this way.

WALDEN POND

Still waiting for a sparrow to light upon my shoulder
Like the one who landed on Henry nearly two centuries ago.
Of course this blessing will never happen to me
Since I fail to invest in sitting still outdoors.

I have journeyed spiritually to this pond more than a few times
And taken some of whom I've loved along as well.
Whether alone or with friends, each visit moves me completely
With every pilgrimage to this famous pond.

Initially I was shocked by the swimming beach and bath house
Near the parking lot, gift shop and scale exhibit of his house.
I've learned to pass these modern invasions and take the trail
As soon as I can to avoid these profane uses of the pond.

Anticipation always builds as I loop the pond to his home site
With rocks pilgrims have piled upon the chain defined spot
In a cove out of sight of the beach. I turn to gaze longingly
On the water as he surely did from his doorstep for two years.

Around a further bend along the trail, in another quiet spot,
I always strip to baptize myself in the cool clear water,
Imagining how he too might have felt along these same shores.
I take a good long dunk, drinking this pond into my very being.

Even though I strive to follow his wisdom in how I live my life,
I know I will never live as simply as he once did here.
But in today's busy world, I strive to live with the grace
That Walden Pond gave to him, and he shared with us.

For my sun, like Henry's long ago, is still but a morning star!

Above the Glacier

Our gentler hike today up to the glacier and lunch beyond
Finished with a tougher climb just before we reached the hut.
Upon arriving we turned to take in a spectacular view of
A trio of snow-capped mountains high above the glacier.

Greatly appreciated were the warm lunch and fresh water.
Before we sat down at picnic tables on the hut porch,
We stood for a long while in awe of the mighty forces
That provided this stunning view above the glacier.

Today's eight-mile round trip journey through an Alpine forest
From the mountain train taking us most of the way there,
Provided many worthwhile views and photos along our hike,
Capped with a final group photo on the porch above the glacier.

This final hike provided a fine conclusion to our week of
Many glorious hikes throughout northern Italy and Switzerland.
And as you and I together lay sweetly in each other's arms tonight and forever,
May we ever dream fondly of this late September hike . . . above the glacier.

Thinking of You My Daughter

As we emerge from the tunnel after a late dinner.
A flute and electric piano share a romantic classic.
High above a "Melissa" moon glows brightly
Over the shining rock in sheltered Montorosso Bay
And I think of you.

Earlier this night our troop hiked many long steps
To the ancient cemetery above St. Francis's chapel:
Fresh flowers adorning more than a few of the crypts.
We climbed to view both sides of this sea-side town
And I thought of you.

Now early this morning a local train broke the stillness
Above these shimmering Mediterranean waters,
Next to the now-deserted beach that is
Shouldered by the back-lit eastern hills.

The town lamps along the walkway to the tunnel
Have just flickered off, the light behind the hills grows brighter.
As I wait for the sun to crest the high ridge,
Turning dawn into day, and we embark on our next journey.
I again think of you.

No matter where we roam or what I witness next,
I will always be thinking of you.

FAMILY

The Kids Are All Right

Hot Wheels for her, piano lessons for him.
Modest encouragement for the sports you each chose,
Reluctant willingness to abandon my own sports dreams.

High expectations: take responsibility for yourselves,
Be generous with others. Take half of your Halloween candy
To the children's hospital, where there are no tricks or treats.

We tried discipline by natural consequences,
But how many mistakes did we make?
More, I'm sure, than I now care to admit.

Times when our own needs drove parenting choices
—careers and financial worries ever present—
When some expectations were clearly unfair.

Yet even in today's less forgiving world
Both of you turned out all right,
Though differently than we ever dreamed

Despite all our fears and expectations.
Please forgive us for all our parenting mistakes
And take pride yourselves in how you each have grown.

Know too that we are both so proud of you—
The persons and adults you are today—
And thank you for enriching our family.

Love, Dad

Looking Forward

Roaring dimly lit tunnel
Through the night sky,
Broken by infant shrieks and
The no-longer-glorified steward:
"Just ice water please," I reply.

Wonder what I really want
Knowing for sure it is not
On this rolling cart or even
Anywhere in this crowded tin can,
Nor likely to be found on this journey.

Too tired to attempt sleep
Though I need the rest.
Breaking my usual routine should help
But this trip is always tough,
Even with a favorable forecast.

Trying to reach across the wide canyon
Of our very different lives,
Our opposing roles,
Is never easy for either of us
Even when each tries his level best.

To prepare I again remind myself:
Don't plan or even expect much.
Try to just be present with him.
Ask and wait for his non-response,
Then listen all the more for what is not said.

I was so looking forward
To visiting my son
Yesterday.

Three Long Days Visit

Our visit pleasant enough,
Just feels so sad:
Three days much harder
Than phone calls weekly.

Minimal expectations are dashed
During our very first meal
Shortened by hasty retreat—
Crowded restaurant too stressful.

A shared constant quandary:
How much activity isn't
Too much for him
Yet enough for me?

So each day we
Part early to recover,
To deal with disappointments,
To gird for tomorrow.

Still wish for more
Then again check myself,
For more cannot be—
Not now, maybe never.

Merry Christmas my son.

Measures

Minus nine this morning on an arbitrary scale
Then suddenly more than seventy inside the terminal.
Makes for interesting clothing choices
As I wait for more than sixty on another numeric scale.

This largely successful trip to visit my son
Has had its own extremes too,
But on less measurable dimensions of
Hope, loss, boredom and resignation.

Indeed this was one of our better visits
With positive indicators clearly evident:
I met a new resident friend for my son,
Pleasant exchanges between us throughout our time together,
Easy-going logistics (once I stopped trying to plan them).
In short, he was the best I have seen him in years.

I'm truly grateful for every one of these.
Yet I can't help feeling what a sad life my son leads—
Currently and for his foreseeable future—
Until unpredictably and suddenly his life will again become
much worse.

I tell myself on my way home to hold on to this visit
With these most variable of all human scales,
Where numbers and measures are nearly as impossible
As this attempt to describe my conflicting feelings.

Horizonless View

Endless wet grey tarmac
An even greyer sky,
Dense fog blends the two:
A good winter day in Minnesota.

More than an hour to departure
If the flight remains on time,
Then a three-hour layover
Before my final flight home.

Mimics the last three long days
Visiting my disabled son:
A lot of waiting and moderate
Fog between the two of us.

Calm conversations since we
Avoided anything important.
His future as blank as
This horizonless view.

Shortened daylight fits
Our lack of any agenda,
Enabling too much screen time
For each of us—our only escape.

Important to have seen him, support him,
Even if I die some each visit.
Hope I sleep the first leg home
To put all this greyness behind me.

Haiku for You

    Transitions are hard
To comprehend and do well
      Yet still we must try.

              ※

      Miss you very much
Need you to miss me some too—
       Let us fix this soon.

              ※

      Remember the days
After we first met when we
    Swore we'd never part?

              ※

      Let's recreate them
Anew for a second time
   Slower this time 'round.

              ※

      When this is over
Let's go for a good long walk
     Together again.

              ※

    Come back to our bed
Let me roll you in my arms,
     Touch you forever.

From One Man to One Woman
(after viewing the video *From Women to Men*)

I too am sorry.
Sometimes it feels my cultural duty is
To act first or speak first, then be sorry.
This time I really mean it.

Unfairly I expect you to want what I want.
And I put my needs ahead of yours—
Like me driving when you want to drive,
Like you making dinner because you cook better.

After years together we fall into habits—
Patterns, clothes all too familiar.
I respect our different interests but get jealous of yours,
Wonder why you aren't more interested in mine.

I admire your endless nurturing
Even long after our chicks have flown.
You challenge me to become better too:
Clearly there is much to improve.

You are strong, intelligent and beautiful
More than you ever realize
Which makes you even more enticing,
Makes me even more fortunate.

I do think of what you want, what you feel
In part because of my many advantages.
And we clearly are at our best
When we act as a team, as partners.

But I often push my own agenda ahead of yours.
I should let you lead or just decide for us both.
Not delegation but outright respect for your choices—
Show that I trust your instincts and values.

So, I really am sorry for assuming
We both always want the same things.
And especially for not always loving you
The way you wish to be loved.

I will do better:
Because you deserve it,
Because I should be there for you,
Because I love you.

LIVING WITH IT

The harshness of her persistent winter cough grips
us both.
Even after twelve years the worry for each of us
persists.
A week delay between an episodic mammogram and results—
interminable.
Yet when the all-clear finally arrives, we silently remain
skeptical.

The fear remains too great.

So instead I hold your hip and cuddle you when I come to bed
later.
Soon the king bed provides plenty of room to sleep and wake
separately.
Life goes on as we choose not to deal with this fear
every day.
Rather we learn to accept the probability of recurrence despite
the results.

The fear never really goes away.

You said never again to chemo and radiation even if it
returns.
And we both know what that means should it ever
recur.
So, most of the time we avoid talking about that
eventuality.
And decidedly don't plan for it should it ever
return.

We learn to live with the fear.

There is simply nothing else to do.

Between the Sheets

Sheets of heavy rain
cocoon us under thick blankets:
you gently snoring,
my hand on your hip
between the flannel sheets.

Our warmth now so intense
I roll onto my back,
sigh deeply and wonder:
whatever became of that even
more intense fire between us?

In Venice

The water bus slowly transported us
from the rail station to Rialto:
we both enjoying the facades and colorful flower boxes
all along the Grand Canal in Venice.

Our quiet lunch along a back canal
unhurried and far from the bustling humanity
cramming the major throughways and
narrow twisting streets in Venice.

Now dense fog early this morning
reveals only a few stars in the
moonless sky while we wait at the station
for the bus to the airport in Venice.

I'm still glowing from our last full day in Europe,
relatively unscheduled, leaving time for just the two of us:
making love with you l a n g u i d l y
on our 29th anniversary . . . in Venice.

Preventative Maintenance

scattered
                        free-floating

             smeared
                                              disjointed

using white liquid car wax on the midnight-blue surface
cleans and shines much better than on my pearl-white older car,
though they equally exhaust me waxing them across two days.
and yet it's the newer blue hood that shows stone marks more,
requiring more touch-up paint that never looks quite right.

beautiful
                                                                cruel
                   selfish

             engaging

no matter how hard I woo you after all these years
you feign so little interest in me or my body—how can that be?
so why do I desire you and your body so intensely still
or is it merely desire itself that I seek in vain?
after all we've been through together—or maybe that itself is the problem.

failed
             ugly
                                                         old
             foolish

what else am I to think?

Will He?

Will he continue to attend
My symphony chorus concerts and
Midnight masses at All Souls Episcopal
To faithfully support my one true love—singing?

Will he still love me
Should my breast cancer return?
For I swore I'd never do chemo again, no matter what;
But after ten years I just don't know. Does he?

Will he still need me
To cook healthy meals, to mend his clothes
And his body after his next bike accident?
Or will he get others to readily help with such tasks?

Will he hold me closely every night
As we fall asleep in our too-large bed?
Will he stroke me tenderly down there
When I turn sleeping most soundly on my back?

Will he still want me
Even though I rarely need or want him as I once did?
We share our bed for sleep and to watch TV together;
After all this time isn't that enough for him too?

Will he still remember our good times
As I continue to lose my more recent memories
Or when I make mistakes he has to correct?
When my near certain medical fear finally fully arrives?

Will he stay with me
When the stress of our two adult children and their illnesses
Becomes finally too much for us to bear any further?
When exhausted and spent we simply decide no more?

Will he remain a part of me,
Part of my very being,
When I now remember that
He is already long gone?

Thirty Years

Much shared across our thirty married years:
Dual careers with interruptions and changes,
Risked all to jointly create a unique business then let it go,
Financial worries before eventual success.

Raised two children to now fine adults:
Severe mental illness in one nearly destroyed us,
The other too-long estranged yet recently re-found;
Now we foster an infant son to start it all over again.

Two religions with mutual respect for both,
Scrimping, saving and spending off budget,
Severe accidents, breast cancer and long recoveries:
Doubts and worries paired with joys and triumphs.

Shared values with too much bickering on the small stuff;
Big dreams and plans—some met but many let go.
Travels together and apart, strains beyond measure,
But always there for each other no matter what.

Respect, love, admiration, and sleeping together
Yet plenty of challenges to each other and ourselves.
What a long strange trip it has been and I
Thank you for being my partner through it all.

Happy Anniversary my love—dare we attempt thirty more?

GRATITUDE

We were so different
On so many levels,
It is quite amazing
That I came from you.

Maybe that is why
There was so much pain,
So much anguish when often
We disappointed each other.

You taught me to be responsible,
To take care of my younger brothers,
To never play the victim card
That you so often played.

You taught me to work hard
And always do good work
So as not to end up
As bitter as you.

I could not be there
When you left this world—
Not for you then nor for me—
And that I sometimes regret.

But in so many ways
You must have done your best;
And you certainly sacrificed much
Raising your four boys.

So now I thank you, Mom,
For your many sacrifices,
For your conditional love,
For who you were, and most of all

For teaching me not to become you.

Jim Carillon

Along Mogadore Road

I smelled burning leaves today the first time in decades:
It brought me back to my childhood years and the joy
Of staying with my grandparents on Mogadore Road
As a retreat from our own chaotic house for a few days.

Inside was her domain since he worked rotating shifts:
Helping her make creamed chicken over fresh biscuits,
Me snaking dominos on the white-tiled fireplace hearth,
Sleeping upstairs in a big bed under the slanted roof.

But outside was Grandpa's world of influence:
Me climbing the pussy willow tree in the back yard,
Rummaging through his garage at the back of the lot,
And us raking leaves along Mogadore Road.

We'd rake from the steps up to their tall front porch
All the way to the ditch between the two giant elm trees
That flanked their property along Mogadore Road.
Grandpa let me jump in the piles before he lit the fire

Next to the road. With the smoke rising before us,
We inhaled that pungent smell of burning leaves,
Watching the fire with a hose nearby—just in case—
Admiring all we'd accomplished while having such fun.

Now I would never burn the leaves I rake each fall
Avoiding carbon it would add to already challenged air.
I must confess I really miss that enticing smell and those
Halcyon days of burning leaves along Mogadore Road.

Thanks Dad

Thanks Dad for modeling and sharing your enthusiasm for sports:
Your love for each game and how to be an effective team player.
Taking me to see a Cleveland Browns game and hometown HS championships.
Showing me how to punt the football high so your team gets there before the ball lands.
Teaching me how to field a grounder, slide into second, throw a curve ball.
Coaching me in golf and in life how to keep my head down and follow through.
In basketball and in life track not the points you score but of the number of assists you make.

Thanks Dad for teaching me to manage my own economic destiny:
Earn your success by working hard and always looking for ways to improve.
Avoid all debt; work and save to buy my first car with cash at 17.
How vital a good education has been throughout my varied careers.
Work my way through college and grad school, graduating with only one student loan.
Invest in my future early and enough to retire earlier than I ever planned.
And thanks Dad for teaching me to live within our means to provide for my family.

Thanks Dad for teaching me to live my values even when they differed from yours:
Work as hard as a husband and father as a worker for someone else.
When you receive an unexpected gift, share it widely with others.
Investing in my church and faith is an investment I'll never regret.
Helping others is why we are put on this earth.

For these and so many other life lessons all I can say is, "Thanks Dad!"

Jim Carillon

Holding Cell Visit

Tiny holding cells fronted by short driveways
Filled with one large vehicle in the carport
Or empty for those still up north during the holiday.

Postage stamp lawns proudly displaying the American flag
Or a favorite college team or maybe a state-of-origin sign
So you know from whence they all have come.

Conversations about which neighbor down the street
Is struggling with which disabling disease
Or lost a life-long spouse two months ago.

A few walkers leashed to their dogs
Strolling along the narrow asphalt paths
Used primarily by others in golf carts.

No parking on the street itself so
We park in the neighbor's drive instead—
She may not make it back to the park so soon.

My father haggard, not eating much these days,
Sleeps in his tip-up chair so he can get help up
With another's hand to use his walker to the bathroom.

He the Renaissance athlete, once All-State in basketball,
Is barely the shell of his active self. Once my model for life,
Now fades in and out of naps all day before going to bed.

His cell sweltering yet he complains that it is just too cold
And hollers at his wife about changing the thermostat:
She can't do anything enough and yet does too much for him.

I am so frightened by this visit to this flat wasteland,
Hoping against all hope that this holding cell purgatory
Will end soon for Dad and NOT be my fate one day.

FAREWELL FATHER

I guess we shouldn't be surprised.
You have hustled and fought your whole life,
Been the most tenacious competitor,
Taught all your boys to work hard like you.

So now it is the cancer you battle
Growing in your very bones,
Taking away everything from you,
And still you fight on.

We try to comfort you, both from near and far,
Help you keep some semblance of dignity,
But it is such a losing battle
And it just prolongs your terrible misery.

It's OK to let go anytime now Dad,
For we all know you've done your best.
What do you really have left but
Pain and hardship for both you and us?

Time for the showers after this final contest
And us celebrating the glory of your accomplishments.
We all know you did such a fine job
With almost everything you touched.

Farewell and God speed to your final rewards.

Sudden Departure

What do I do now
That you are gone
My model, my guide,
My beloved father?

We never thought you'd last this long
Given your steep decline since Thanksgiving.
This awful end, long anticipated and now here,
Is still a great shock.

Not even one last trip
To see you before you died:
Just hours before my flight today
You left before I could depart.

I never got to share the poem
That I wrote last week imploring you
That it was OK now to let go;
I guess you knew this yourself.

I will miss you more than I can say.

STARTLING IMAGE

While vacationing with family on a beach in Florida
I was wiping down my new car with the shammy
When suddenly I was startled by my father's image
Right there on the hood of my recently waxed car.

His image so very clear to me, right down
To the wide black T-shirt, white shorts with
Dark belt, white athletic socks, and of course,
The obligatory team-logo ball cap on his head.

There he was, just staring up at me:
Dragging the shammy carefully across the hood
Then wringing it out thoroughly until nearly dry,
Just the way he taught me many years ago.

But how can this be—his image on the hood?
We lost him to cancer eight months ago,
His passing a blessing after his gaunt look
And eventual loss of dignity by the end.

Today his image not slight at all—heavy even—
And certainly looking strong enough for another lesson
On the importance of keeping your car looking nice
With the essential final shammy wipe down.

Good to see you again, Dad; I look forward to
Being with you again during my next car wash!

Guiding Light in Absentia

What would your father have done
In these troubled times, my wife asks?
I guess like the rest of us he might have
Down played the trouble at first.

Nothing much slowed him down until
His very end: denial as a key strategy.
He often told me: when it gets tough,
The tough just get going.

But by now even he would be cautious.
Safety and personal responsibility were
Important values that he also taught me,
And he was all for helping others.

So, for Dad and for the next generations
We each keep a safe distance and wear a mask
Even as we stay active in both work and play,
Living outdoors as much as we can.

I miss him so much even though I'm glad
He did not share this current national horror.
I just hope I can teach his values and sense
To my kids as well as he did for me.

Graduation Day
(A vivid remembrance brought by a dream)

All of us siblings and
A few close friends were
Gathered on the wide front porch
Of that sacred place that

Had nurtured each of us
In varying ways, yet prepared
All of us well for our vastly
Different journeys to come.

Some of us had returned from a great distance
To celebrate our youngest sibling's graduation.
It would be years before we all gathered again
For a sadder reason next time.

Our youngest wore her bright summer dress
So colorful against these blue hills.
She looked so sweet, so young, so ready
For whatever her next steps might be.

Raucous conversations had flowed freely
With the ritual sibling teasing of our youth.
But then the moment became quiet enough to hear
The babbling creek swelled with yesterday's rain.

I laid my unopened book at my feet as there
Would be plenty of time to read on the flight home.
We all embraced this rare softer moment,
Perhaps each aware of how special it had become.

Now many years later in the early quiet of this morning,
The late-May streams swelled again with heavy rain,
The birds happily announce this bright new day
Even though the sun has not yet cleared the ridge.

Angels Landing
December 1, 2018

Today of all days
my faded green T-shirt
simply says Angels Landing—
last year's severe climb.

Today's journey tougher still,
witnessing these panels again—
The Names Project Quilt
on World AIDS Day.

So many fallen angels,
my brother among them
gone nearly thirty years—
still miss him greatly.

Despite all their differences—
why couldn't we see
them ALL as angels
while still among us?

Next time brother
come some other day—
today spread your wings
and fly my brother fly.

Your Favorite Song
"Have you ever seen the rain coming down some sunny day?"
—Creedence Clearwater Revival

Whenever I hear this song, I think of you:
You so loved their music early on
And because you loved them I could not.

In other ways I would choose X and you would choose Y.
What I didn't realize then was our many differences
Were so much deeper than sibling rivalry.

I'm ashamed to say it took years for me to realize this
And longer still to really appreciate our differences.
I shudder to think how badly I treated you.

Not even naming my beloved son after you and your partner
Will ever compensate for how I behaved back then,
Will fill the hole in my heart for you, will ever bring you back.

Maybe honoring you, remembering your favorite music,
And learning to appreciate others different from me
Will at least keep some part of you in my life.

Thank you, brother, for just being you.
Please know that finally I too have since
Seen the rain coming down some sunny day.

Family Portrait

The stark white marble of the Washington Monument provides the backdrop for our not so merry band of worldly travelers—including Stanley and his father from here in DC, all the way to Joe from the Mission District of San Francisco. Aline and I drove up from Richmond and Joe's niece in from Maryland. Our stern faces shout at the photographer, belying the multitude of feelings we've all experienced since early that morning.

The solemnity of the unfolding ceremony at dawn—the quiet reverence, the careful stepping and drawing out of the folded panel squares, the loving circling of the panels unfurled, and the placing of each square so gently on the ground—still lingers in my mind and heart despite the enormity and chaos since. Now the sheer vastness of the display covering the entire DC Mall in both directions can only begin to be revealed on this knoll by the Washington monument behind us. This endless rectangle of all these displayed squares, and all the panels within, rolls through every witness like thunder. The enormity worries us about what this will mean for each of us going forward. The sheer collective weight of all that has already occurred, the sadness so many of us have long endured. How long must this go on for our entire nation, for the world? Clearly this is madness on full display.

I draw my wife closer, arm in arm, hoping we can be there for each other despite our pain. Yet this day I have little left to give her. This gesture is probably more about what I need than what I can provide. Then I feel her simply respond in kind as if to say, "Yes, I understand."

Joe shows me his list of names of the panels he has come to find in this sea of suffering. I too have my own list but mine is much shorter. Joe's list must be 50 names or more—how can that be? (Later he tells me there are 67 names on his list.) I don't even know 67 people in my life as close as Joe who knew and loved each one, including the one name on both of our lists: his partner and my brother, Jeff.

Yet all of us witnessing this display are there to remember them, to remember their names, ALL their names. And for each of us, our own memories of the direct connections we have with some of these names. Despite this vast display of the awful carnage, each panel captures a little of someone we each have loved and lost. From this hill the long display shows undeniably the diversity and beauty of this nearly endless multi-colored ribbon tying us all together, the many colors blurring through our tears.

Jeff, your panel has memories from each member of our family, however painful and unwilling we found this task to be. How do you choose a memory, a picture, or a few words to capture what you have meant to each of us and then add our own small contribution to this memorial? What could I possibly say about my brother who was both difficult at times and crucial to who I am today? How do I capture the myriad feelings to add to this baby-blue background that our mother picked for you? Somehow, we each did it, adding our unique memory to each of these simple three-by-six-foot cloth panels.

This day, Jeff, you were here among many thousands of others who died to convince the world that we must stop this madness. We all must help end this horrific disease of AIDS, before the Names Project Quilt covers the whole world. Let it begin with us, let it begin with me.

And on this very day, next to this monument, Aline and I decided to enlarge our family through adoption. After another challenging journey for the next year, a three-month old beautiful son entered our lives: Jeffrey Joseph, named in honor of you and Joe.

Now nearly 30 years on know that I still miss you so much my brother, especially because you are NOT in this picture by the monument. But also know that this framed family portrait without you in it, still hangs lovingly on our bedroom wall with all our other family photos. Sleep well tonight my brother.

Jim Carillon

Exercising Body and Mind

Jim Carillon

COOL WHEELS!
ANNOUNCING THE DUAL-SPORT HYBRID

Girls love the flaming red color and sleek design—
Low to the ground, so little wind resistance.
Yet amazing visibility—you'll never see more:
Simply envelops you in the world in which you are driving.

Powered by efficient and silent dual piston engineering—
Requiring no fossil fuels, no exhausts—simply runs on water!
No clutch yet twenty-seven gears so smooth
You shift the transmission with a flick of a finger.

Amazingly quick starts—be first through any intersection.
Maintenance and repairs—few and inexpensive.
Infinite mileage range; fits in any parking spot.
Costs so little no lease is required.

Automatic air conditioning each time you crest a hill.
Huge sunroof, disk brakes and Halogen lights front and rear.
Driving so fun: feel the wind rushing, your pulse quickening,
First six months driving it I couldn't stop and lost 20 pounds!

The ultimate machine for loving every journey!
Care to take it for a spin?

THE SECOND SUMMIT

It was my idea to hike the Mist Trail to
Two separate waterfalls—Vernal and Nevada—
Climbing 2000 feet to their summits.

Stunning views all along our journey,
Thoroughly soaked by Vernal's mist
While ascending its 600 steep stone steps.

After resting my bad ankle at this first crest
And knowing our return would be just as challenging,
We three pushed on toward Nevada's summit.

Following the overflowing river, witnessing its immense power,
We climbed onward and crossed the footbridge
With more great views without much difficulty.

Then just above Nevada's thundering base
Mist again enveloping us as we climbed,
My ankle began to hurt with every step.

Hoping I retained enough strength for the two hours down,
I admitted defeat and stopped a while to draft these lines
While Dave and Phil climbed onward to the second summit.

Ashamed of not reaching the second summit myself
Yet thankful for all the wonders seen along this journey,
I can't wait to hike Yosemite again tomorrow.

Fortunate Fairview Foragers

To Tater Knob's lookout there are two paths we can take:
The usual that shadows the creek on the west side part way,
The other that hops rocks and crosses this constant stream
More than a few times before we arrive at Crawdad falls.

Given the recent rain we chose the latter
But had to bushwhack our way back to the former,
The creek so swelled that we could not cross this morning
Without wading to our knees at each crossing.

We then closely hugged the creek toward the falls,
With the water so full, more thunderous than ever.
Instead of following the trail westward to the overlook,
We bushwhacked our way southward staying closer to the stream.

Amazed at the unusual rushing glory of this water
We chose—no, we dared not—leave the stream just yet.
The partial path we followed quickly dwindled,
Forcing us to weave around the plentiful Rhododendron.

Before we reached the next four-foot water fall
I looked up at eyes' height to find a single horseshoe
Grown right into a notch in another Rhododendron tree
So firmly that I could not budge it at all.

Did a rider set it here long ago
When this tree was surely much smaller?
For clearly the tree grew right through this shoe,
Incorporating it into its very being.

How lucky we are today to witness this surprise—
One of many we encounter on Tuesday mornings
As we climb these hills and often find unusual treasures,
Whether we make it to the next lookout or not.

Does this shoe portend the reclaiming of the earth
When our finite human existence someday ends?
Will the forest just take over all our human efforts,
Like kudzu burying an abandoned farm truck?

Or is this just today's sign of our great fortune
In taking these hikes together each week,
Sharing our stories, discovering each other
And the many natural wonders we witness every walk?

Either way, this horseshoe brings me hope after all.

Jim Carillon

Making My Own Breezes

I so enjoy riding my bicycle early in the morning
With some light but before the sun crests the ridges.
My path fully shaded for at least the ride out,
The cooler morning air refreshing me round trip.

I head mostly eastward then later to the north
To the roadside spring just beyond the divide.
Up four distinct hills on the way to this spring,
I climb almost all the way there from home.

Heading eastward at this hour I am often delighted
As I was again this clear morning, to see not one
But a handful of sunrises as I crest each ridge,
The sun heralding the day anew each time it bursts over the trees.

The climbing is hard but more than worth it,
Sweat pouring off my body in buckets.
As I crest each hill and again pick up speed,
I make my own breezes on the shorter downhill runs.

Enjoying these breezes against my sweat soaked skin,
Cooling me thoroughly, I shudder with tingly delight.
Downhill I fly, seemingly soaring like the birds,
Cool air rushing by my ears and across my limbs.

Two wild turkeys dart across the road as I bend a curve
Just before the spring pipe juts from the hillside.
The water so cool, so refreshing; I gulp it heartily
Then refill my bottle for more on my way home.

Turning back westward and again up the toughest hill
The prevailing westerly wind now refreshes me anew
Even though my pace slows on this serious climb.
Cars and pick-up trucks again pass me in their greater rush.

Hearing one behind me I signal to go around by curving my left arm.
Not one but two trucks roar by as they accelerate up the hill
Dashing across the double yellow line again into our lane
Just before another oncoming car quickly approaches.

I know their pace doesn't permit them to notice
The glorious songbirds or the fog lifting from the shimmering lake.
An old weathered barn now in full sun stands proudly in the valley
Where earlier it hid shrouded in the then foggy field.

The wayside pulpit next to the Baptist church atop Chestnut Hill
Though sometimes witty is not nearly as convincing as this
Babbling brook, the endless vegetation and these beautiful mountains
That clearly there is something greater than any of us here.

As I dismount to walk my bike up our shared steep driveway
My neighbor rolls down his window as he rolls down our drive.
He is going out to chase the little white ball and says to me,
"Looks like you're having fun." I breathlessly reply, "Yes indeed!"

Bill if you only knew what a joy it has been
For over two hours this glorious morning,
Biking up and over these wondrous hills
And in so doing, making my own breezes.

Cloudy Days

Another cloudy winter day,
Storms forecast again this afternoon.
Where are all the blue skies
For which this area is known?

Yesterday morning's group hike
Cancelled again due to rain.
Have we all become too soft,
Letting weather decide for us?

Returning to songs from my youth
I crave those younger feelings again:
The hauntingly familiar, the known
During these stormier times.

"And a song I was writing is left undone,"
Calls to me especially these days.
For I also leave much undone with
Less time left in which to do it.

Get moving I tell myself,
No need to wait for clearing skies.
Start the journey regardless of the weather,
The sun shall return soon enough.

NOT WAITING

I'm not very good at waiting
But maybe I could at least say hello
To a friend waiting at the bus stop
For the campus shuttle up the hill.

We briefly chat this sunny morning.
The shuttle to the classroom building
Still nowhere in sight so I decide
To walk the steep hill instead.

The sun warms me as the grade first increases,
Eases some, then sharply increases again.
Endless cars whizzing by are flagged by
A mobile meter flashing their speed.

(I walk too slowly for it to register my gait.)
Fewer birds than expected this wintry morn
Despite today's glorious break in the weather.
Two shuttles now have passed me as I climb.

I still arrive at the classroom
Long before most of the others,
Take a seat and peel an orange—
My lunch today which I slowly savor.

I would have arrived even earlier
Had I waited for the shuttle at the bus stop,
But would have missed this morning's amble
And the joy of stretching my legs and my mind.

35-KM RIDE TO LAKE BOLSENA

Yesterday I rode a bicycle for the first time in weeks—
It felt so good to be on the road again this way.
The rolling hills of Umbria were challenging enough,
Riding four hours to this distant lake and back.

In early October these hillsides were largely barren
With wide rural vistas and some unusual trees.
Traffic was light once I climbed the long rise
Heading south out of Orvietto to Balsena.

Bolsena Lake is immense and with today's wind
Three-foot waves crashed the shoreline in town.
This southern wind was in my face during this long uphill climb—
Without a stop I ran out of water on the way back—gasp!

Exhausted and so very thirsty by ride's end,
Still the views of the elevated town of Orvietto
With its immense castle walls placed on top of its own
High plateau is amazing from the southern hillside.

Such a ride made for an especially sound sleep last night.

This Time Just for Me

Today's second bicycle ride this week from Orvietto was easier,
This time the wind was out of the north helping my climb.
Journeying south-eastwardly to Bagnoregia also seemed less steep
And I cut my planned route by not going to Lubriano as well.

In short, I chose to be easier on myself for a change.
When I arrived at a wonderful overlook of the Civitá di Bagnoregia,
I took some pictures of this ancient city on the hill instead of descending
To the valley below and walking the long entry ramp into the Civitá itself.

I'd seen enough ancient walled cities on high plateaus
And certainly enough of the many Catholic churches within,
Not to mention the crowded cobblestone streets with endless
Retail establishments that I would never enter anyways.

Now I relax in an outdoor café in Orvietto waiting for lunch.
My traveling companions sit elsewhere soaking in a hot spring.
Instead I walked 10 km to town then rode at least 30 km
From Orvietto to the lookout at Bagnoregio and back again.

Soon I'll catch my breath, let my sweat-soaked back dry,
Pay too much for a nice grilled fish but all is simply fine.
This day was just for me and I have earned these calories.
Today I will even buy a Gelato on my way back to the inn!

Against the Wind

I've written before of my joy of
Choosing to ride my bicycle when I commute.
Here I share the challenges of riding
My bike on an especially windy day.

My usual 13-mile journey to church yesterday
Was brisk but I had bundled enough for the cold.
Only my gloved hands were chilled on the downhill runs,
The rest of me warm from multiple layers.

I noticed some shimmy in my wheels on the first downhill:
Leaving late this morning I forgot to pump my tires before I left.
I stopped and sure enough the rear tire pressure was low
But I thought I had enough air to at least get me to church.

The climbing of the four hills on this route was tougher due to
Less tire pressure resulting in me arriving a little later than usual.
The stiff wind from the north-west a definite challenge,
Slowing me as I turned northward on Route 9 to the gap.

After church, the wind had picked up considerably and
Shifted to coming almost directly from the west.
This stiffer wind now sideswiping me up the return climb
Southward this same long hill to Lackey Gap.

When I turned right after coming down this long hill
The wind was now directly into me the rest of the way.
At times on the next gentle rise it felt like
I was moving backwards into this stiff wind.

Pedaling mostly westward toward home, the steep climb up
The next hill was so intense with heavy wind gusts I had to
Dismount and walk the bicycle up this sharp climb,
Catching my breath as I pushed onward against the wind.

If only I could reach the top of this most elevated climb
Then maybe I could pick up some speed on the sharp downhill
Before climbing immediately again the shorter Chestnut Hill.
But my low tire caused me to pedal even on this downhill run.

With only one more major climb to the next gap
I could hopefully glide the slow descent past Echo Lake
And much of my remaining journey would be mostly downhill.
Too late—exhausted I had to dismount again this last climb.

Finally I pulled into my drive after taking twice as long as usual,
Hardly able to walk my bike up our steep driveway.
As I climbed the stairs to our house I was fully spent and
After showering had to lie flat in bed the rest of the day.

From now on I will also review the wind forecast
And make sure to check and pump my tires every time,
Before I ever embark on another such grueling ride.
Or better yet decide to drive instead of biking against the wind.

What Will It Take?

Cold clear winter morning yet
I move slowly through a fog of
Aches, congestion and coughing,
Every movement a struggle.

When simply putting on socks and shoes
Is a challenge to stay upright,
Then I've clearly waited too long
To get needed medical help.

Nearly a week ago I thought
I could just tough this out.
OK, so I now surrender,
Finally going to see the doctor.

A bad year I'm told,
Others in this state are dropping like flies.
(Strange analogy given it is a cold January.)
But not me for I'm in too good of shape.

Now after a tough week I just want this to end.
Doc just give me a shot, some pills maybe;
I've got too much to do in my busy schedule
Already interrupted by this damn flu.

But too late she says, nothing now can be done
Except bed rest and Advil for the aches.
She and I are each left wondering,
In various ways, what will it take?

Removing Thistles

Finally!
Finished the neglected and over-grown thistle row today,
Digging and pulling weeds for three long shifts.

Hauled a dozen or more barrow loads of
Mostly stinging thistles to the woods to reduce
Their virulent spread in this community garden.

At least this row is now free of these fierce competitors:
We'll next lay a tarp over the row for much needed
Fallow rest before again planting vegetables or flowers.

Beyond the dirt and sweat carried home each night,
And unlike other obligations with less observable outcomes
It feels good to see this clear result of my efforts.

You see the rest of my life is consumed in process,
Hoping my efforts will someday pay dividends:
Only time will tell with much less feedback along the way.

So as strenuous and dirty as this job has been,
I am especially grateful for this now clean garden row
And can now move on to weeding other areas in my life.

Jim Carillon

INTROSPECTION

INTROSPECTION

The time has come
For it to get here.
Not sure what it is,
But it is time.

I am sure I can handle it,
No matter what the issue.
It's the waiting
That's always the toughest.

Managing uncertainty
Has never been my strong suit,
And probably never will be.
Like going deep inside.

That nether realm between
All the urgent actions,
The space between my pillars—
What if there is nothing there?

Twenty-Five or Six Past Four
(Apologies to Chicago, Paul Simon, & Neil Young)

Twenty-five or six past four:
Too damn tired to sleep any more.
Cecilia's alarm at six: she gets up to wash her hair,
As she passes our bed still restless I'm there.

I'm exhausted beyond all reason again
Yet I must get up to do what I've planned.
Retirement isn't what I'd expected to be
But neither am I and now too busy to flee.

Now my calendar's more full than when I worked full time
Commitments seem endless which doesn't seem fine.
Nightmares of missing an appointment or two
If this keeps up what's a retiree to do?

Rust never sleeps and these days neither do I
Stressed by my own choices so why do I try?
Surrendered to a cell phone though I tried to resist
It manages my life now and for that I am pissed.

Maybe vacation before I burn out?
But traveling's just as stressful I shout!
Help me I'm drowning while adding more water
Still sinking, still choosing to run faster and farther.

Jim Carillon

Observed Limits to Personal Control

Oft times I've observed the cards seemingly don't fall my way;
Makes playing interactive hearts interesting to say the least.
For one so concerned with controlling my own outcomes
I say this provides extra challenge to my card playing.

Yet then again pleasant surprises do occur if only
I keep a sharp eye for them and an open heart.
It's the uncontrollable that episodically rescues me
When I least expect it or when I choose to abandon my ego.

As on the hike this morning up the return trail of Kitzuma,
Along the well-travelled, doubly barricaded section of Old 70.
We noticed abundant Jewel Weed with its bright orange
Blossoms that anyone would expect to see in late summer.

Further up and around another curve, the same bush
Not orange as I'd always seen it, but flowering in bright yellow—
As yellow as the August sun, as abundant and yellow as
The many Brown-Eyed-Susans we see along this ancient road.

So amazed to find Jewelweed in this unexpected color
I rejoiced in my discovery as though I was the first ever to find it,
Though this has likely been observed for at least two centuries
When this road was hewn westward through the mountains.

This road long ago abandoned with the building of the interstate
Now cluttered with landslides and banks of heavy Kudzu
Taking over everything, including a favorite wild raspberry patch,
With a fury that this patch no longer yields any harvestable fruit.

Yet this path still delights this now slower walking traveler who
Has little control of the wonders along most other journeys too
If only I slow to observe them along this remote byway.
How many wonders might I yet see around the next bend?

When will I learn to abandon control and just go with the flow?

Today I Am ...

I am the sleek Porsche parked in a handicap space,
And a screeching young girl running bases in a kickball game.
I am forest green rather than the blazing red my wife insisted for our Tesla,
A struggling poet instead of the star athlete that my father was.

I am a tree bent low with luscious fruit waiting to be harvested,
A self-made man who volunteers for the many less privileged.
I am a sated man now endeavoring to be uncomfortable again
To deal with issues I've succeeded for decades to suppress.

I am responsible beyond all expectations, liberally guilty for the luxuries I've earned,
And frequently sure of myself amid my confusions.
I am a good father and husband who still wonders about the girl who got away,
An attentive lover who just wants her to desire me as intensely as I desire her.

I am still wondering who I might become next.

How to Avoid Becoming Comfortably Numb
(Counter-inspired by the Pink Floyd song)

Challenge:
Hike a little longer each day,
Commute mostly by bicycle,
Maintain a healthy diet.

Stretch:
Learn a new language,
Sing solo in front of others,
Teach a subject you dimly know.

Help:
Mentor a teenager,
Teach at middle school,
Parent a foster child.

Serve:
Donate substantially and anonymously,
Directly help people less advantaged,
Become a better partner to your spouse.

Seek:
Embark on your own spiritual quest,
Ask how you wish to be remembered,
Write and share meaningful poems.

Worthy Someday?

Cut from the little-league baseball team
And later eighth-grade basketball.
Skinny teen with ugly glasses and
Self-esteem / identity issues.

College dropout who worked much
To first put wife then self through college
And grad school with little student debt
Long before buying current house debt free.

First love would not even consider me,
Early practice marriage lasted fourteen years.
Current wife and I raised two kids to fine adults,
Now we foster an infant in our late sixties.

Corporate consultant road warrior, frequent flyer,
To support the family and a future
Before creating then selling our own successful
Business for enough to retire in our fifties.

Now a reliable social justice volunteer,
Church leader and frequent blood donor.
Wondering what I yet must accomplish
To be worthy enough someday.

Overcast Day

Drab December day befits my mood—
Something's clearly amiss,
Hiding in the clouds or
Coming soon with the rain.

A troubled nation,
Family issues,
Ache in the lower back.
No, not any of these normal concerns.

Something bigger is afoot—
Like smelling today's rain
Hours before it arrives.
Something brooding, massing.

You must know the feeling:
When things go generally well
For too long this time.
Good can't remain for long.

Better call the kids
Or my father in Florida,
Before the tragedy fully arrives—
Can really sense it getting closer.

What will it be this time?

Worn Identities

The faded light blue *Boogie-Oogies* t-shirt, transparent from too much wearing—
Co-ed softball shirt in grad school from so long ago I can't find the shirt anymore.
Asheville: Cesspool of Sin—What a down-state
politician said of our liberal community.
Shirt worn so proudly for a long time
that the pit-holes became too big;
it's a proud car-wash rag now.

Many reunion T-shirts from my wife's obligatory family gatherings;
Clever sayings with great graphics but I don't relate to them—or the shirts either.
I still regularly and proudly wear
my *Habitat for Humanity* Ts earned
while building an inter-faith home each fall.
So too my *ACA Navi-Gator* T shirt for helping
families for years obtain health insurance.

I Bike AVL—a recent gift starkly black and soft which feels great AFTER a ride;
Pockets on the back of my florescent bike shirts still needed DURING my rides.
Newspaper-sponsored *Give Local!* T
For contributing large donations to
Our local community garden which itself
Is always too cash starved to provide T's
to volunteers, donors or board members.

Sage green T-shirt with *North Face* logo on front, inherited as I myself never buy brand names;
but a soft green color and the brushed texture feels too good not to wear.
With his bold portrait on a green tie-dye
It simply says, *"What Would Thoreau Do?"*
Love this alternative spokesman;
Took church teens to Walden Pond during an
All too rare pilgrimage to this sacred place.

I wear Ts, therefore I am!

Burnout or a New Happiness?

Time to take stock as this busy year
Now draws to an ugly close.
Looking like an even busier year ahead—
Why do I do this to myself yet again?

Should be off-loading rather than adding
During these so-called golden years.
But what to let go of when so many
Worthy causes seemingly need a piece of me?

Even steward leaders need rest,
Causing me to ponder why I continue to push so hard.
Probably that darn identity issue again—
Serving others helps me avoid it for a while.

All the many urgings to become a human being
Rather than be an endless human doing
Haven't convinced or yet taken hold of me:
Stubbornly I refuse to change my behavior.

What is a former consulting psychologist
Supposed to do to heal himself?
Couldn't dare admit to needing to be a client
Who may need another's help, now could I?

Perhaps it is time to seek a new kind of happiness?

Wish Me Luck

Out of sorts
Don't know why;
Missin' you
But you're still here.

Crying child,
Lack of sleep,
Gettin' better
Yet far from calm.

Expect more
But of what?
Others' needs
Often come first.

Keepin' busy
So I don't
Face my own
Needs, desires.

Time to change,
Face myself,
Seek within
What I most need.

Wish me luck.

Be Here Now

Predawn light just enough
To highlight sharp contrasts:
Heavy clouds, light rain,
Fall colors abundant below.

This quiet early morning
Beckons my soul.
Despite today's plans
Conflicting feelings arise.

Need to sit with them:
The feelings, not plans.
Uncertainty not that bad
When I accept it.

Complex world these days,
How much to accept
My personal involvement,
My responsibility to fix?

Maybe today just enjoy
The varied weather,
The glorious contrasts,
Me being here now.

Absence

Too much time on my hands now that you are gone.
The quiet was nice for a short while
but it becomes deafening and endless.
Not something I would ever choose.

What personal choices do we each really make after all?
For one who worships proactive planning,
I assume more personal control than is deserved.
This the foundation on which my successes were built.

Were my achievements as much luck as execution,
or privilege perhaps, aided by gumption early on?
Well-developed habits and work-ethic mean little these days—
my waking hours are now filled with coasting—therefore I am lost.

Still I reach for you, but you are gone.
Remember when we solved transitions together,
leaning on each other, at least one of us providing hope?
There was nothing we couldn't tackle together.

Time now to look within.
And I wonder—is anybody in there?

How Do I?

How do I tell you
when what I have to say
will surely hurt you
no matter how gently I try?

How do I tell myself,
admit what will surely be
so challenging I'll realize
how much I'll have to change?

How do I change my very identity
I've worked so hard to create,
strived so much to project,
core to who I think I am?

Yet then again, how do I not?

PERSONAL AD

Strong enough to bicycle 100 miles a week
Yet weak enough to be passed on climbs by much abler cyclists.
Wealthy enough to no longer worry about my own finances
Yet volunteers tirelessly for the disadvantaged in our community.

Young enough to hike surrounding hills every Tuesday morning
Yet bad ankles and worsening knees mean hobbling after strenuous days.
Undeterred from challenging my limits both physically and emotionally
Yet old enough to show lines and scars from prior risks taken.

Brashly lustful enough to desire attractive women I encounter
Yet wise enough to only act on such fantasies with you.
Disciplined in my day-to-day choices consistent with my values
Yet indulgent with chocolate and carries extra pounds to show for it.

Warmly outgoing and generally healthy in mind, body and spirit
Yet constantly worried about my children's and our country's future.
In short, a man of big appetites and even larger self-expectations
Yet still just making his own way through each day.

Jim Carillon

SOCIAL JUSTICE?

Jim Carillon

Not-So-Empty Buckets

The car wash bucket seems empty
Before I fill it with warm soapy water
To thoroughly wash my two cars weekly,
The way my father taught me.

But before I fill it with water from the sink,
This bucket is not really empty.
History, pride, and sense of family duty
Fill my bucket to overflowing.

I tell folks I just like to drive a clean car,
That it is safer with clear glass in front and back.
But it is a well-earned habit that fills this bucket,
Suds bubbling now with fond memories of Dad.

Just like my race that I rarely choose to think of
Because I still am privileged in so many ways,
This other bucket really is not so empty either
Precisely because I rarely think about my race.

This bucket too is filled with a history of white suburban enclaves
My family moving to progressively better neighborhoods:
"For better schools and resale value," my parents always said.
It's what they didn't say that really drove these moves.

Others in the family, older members mostly, were
Never shy about putting others down with the N-word.
It was their way of saying that at least we have it better than
That other disadvantaged group who has it even worse.

We surely thought we deserved the finer things we earned
With hard work and being careful not to challenge the system.
But putting others down didn't make us any better;
Our buckets just got heavier with such words and our
deference.

Today my privileged bucket remains heavy with regret and guilt
About how little energy I personally devote to challenging
This awful culture and the many systematic injustices still
Designed to make it progressively worse for so many people.

So today I fill my bucket in the sink with water and suds
Hoping to wash away at least some of this cultural dirt
To make the world I drive and live in a little bit better
Or at least the glass a little clearer for us all to see.

Grab a sponge or shammy and join me.

If I Were King ...

If I were king high school girls would be the ones expected to ask high school boys (or girls) to the prom on the condition that any person asked would be required to:
1. Say yes and take the person who first asked you to the prom,
2. Find out what she/he would enjoy most about that night, and
3. Make sure the other person would have a great time.

If I were king auto manufacturers would be required to only produce and sell cars that:
1. Exceeded the fuel efficiency of the current most fuel-efficient car in that class,
2. Not cheat on the fuel efficiency tests, and
3. Cost less than the current most efficient car in that class.

If I were king groceries would be free for anyone whose weight was at the healthy BMI index or less, and health care would be universally available and paid by the government. Taxes to support all this:
1. Everyone pays a straight 7% Federal income tax regardless of income (no tax loopholes),
2. 50% Federal tax on all capital gains for anyone with greater capital gains than mine, and
3. 90% Federal tax on all incomes above what a local public middle school teacher is paid.

If I were king all politicians would be limited to two terms and not receive a salary but rather must pay every constituent $1/year unless:

1. Their constituents had 80% or higher voter participation rate during the last election,
2. Average Incomes and number of employed were both increased over the prior year, and
3. They could accurately describe their political opponents' positions on proposed legislation.

If I were king there would be bike lanes on EVERY road during all uphill portions of the road, and:

1. Wide vehicles (semi's, dump trucks, SUV's) would pay an additional wide lane use tax,
2. Drivers who act like only they own the roads would be forced to only bike for a month, and
3. Winds would be required to blow in the same direction as any bike rider going up a long hill.

If I were king the arc of justice would bend to a straight horizontal line next year by having:

1. All people care about and help those less advantaged than themselves,
2. All of us do at least one thing for someone else anonymously every day, and
3. All adults teach all our children honesty, kindness, and compassion (or better yet learn these things from our children).

White Privilege

In southeast Michigan
If you don't feel the wind
Then it's at your back,
For it's always there.

So often we don't feel it,
Don't see it, don't hear it,
But we can almost taste it
If we stop and notice.

Don't tell me it's not there.
We just don't want to admit it,
Believing instead that our success is
Our own making since we struggled some.

Clearly not as much as others have,
But that doesn't matter. Surely *our success*
Comes from our intelligence, education
And willingness to work hard.

We so want to believe that—
That what we got, we earned.
Why else is there so much
Difference in outcomes?

Or maybe the wind is just at our backs.

Reno Baby!

Tonight's casino tour in Reno bombards all my senses—
The noise, the lights, the smoke, the temptations!
An extravagant dinner in a private back room
Then illusionists show all too metaphorical.
I personally can't wait to escape into sleep.

Quieter morning in a guest suite provides me time to write
Then smooth-as-glass boat ride on nearby Lake Tahoe—
Comparing coveted wooden crafts and lakeside castles
Before expensive lunch at a nearby beach resort,
Reliving memories of a local western TV show.

This immersion into a much higher tax bracket troubles me
As I slide into the leather seat of a custom Mercedes,
As we continue to spend money as if it never matters.
We verbally jab each other to prove our net worth
While trying to respect the life choices we each have made.

I wonder about those not present who struggled much
To enable all the luxuries we are now consuming,
Me struggling to enjoy them now with these other guys.
Why can't I just join in this masculine revelry or at least
Be a more grateful guest in this foreign world?

BUILDING A SAFER WORLD

In your class you scared us for sure.
We all wanted to understand these issues better
But the technical details overwhelmed me
And our sorry state of this world depressed us all.

Rather than empowered we are stuck—
Stuck in the knowledge and awful responsibility.
Without our own weapons to get rid of these
I feel as helpless as the more ignorant are loud.

Our own country's leader is all-the-more frightening
With his stupidity even greater than his bluster.
The rogue state is now us, among many others,
With bellicose infants as leaders on many sides.

The simplicity of an earlier time has long past;
The awful genie has long escaped the bottle.
"All we are saying, is give peace a chance"
Seems as distant as John is dead—murdered no less.

Next time you offer this class spend the last session
On brainstorming ways each of us can respond,
How we might even remotely influence these issues
And walk away with something we can each do.

Or we might as well begin building shelters and hide.

The Leaders We Deserve

Give us simple easy answers
That we don't have to think about
Or work for
Or that ask us to change.

Tell us that you care about us
That you will easily deliver what we want
That things will only get better for us;
Tell us lies if you have to—we expect them.

Make it someone else's fault
That things have been so awful
That some others are to blame;
That stopping them will make it better for us.

Bring back the good old days
When our kind held all the cards,
That we alone deserve the very best
And the hell with all the rest.

Promise us anything:
Give it to us and
Deliver it yesterday.
Show us we're worth it.

Make America Great Again (for us anyways.)

Weathering the Storm

Rumbling storms across our cherished land:
Downpours of lies with every drop,
Thunder and lightning with each new turn,
And nearly half of us just turning our heads.

All advantages go to the advantaged,
Those struggling feeling the most pain.
Delays and blunders make a deadly sickness worse,
Death toll increasing thousands each day.

Like some I too remain paralyzed by fear—
Glued to the tv with each new tragedy.
Trying also to avoid giving an invisible bug
To anyone I might by chance encounter.

Focusing on family while sequestered at home,
Hoping at least to protect our youngest.
Yet I remain lost as to how best to weather
This pandemic of unknowable duration.

How much will we all change to survive?

INSIGNIFICANCE

It's not enough
That this life is hard,
Harder than it ever should be;
But that we make it even harder
By our indifference.

But to lose all hope
That not only it will
Never get any better,
But that you'll leave no legacy
When this tough life is done.

Makes me wonder again
What legacy I am leaving,
What I'm willing to yet do
To stand with someone else
Before it's too late for me too.

Or maybe there's no escape for either of us.

MALADAPTING

Lines radiating like clock hands:

- Or together we can never again look eye to eye.
- Either I and we must get ourselves together
- Now seems more uncertain than either.
- Past is gone, future remote, there is only now --
- Wrong-headed in hoping this too will soon pass.
- Anyone can tell something is terribly wrong,
- Being restless and not of much use to anyone.
- Endlessly searching for how to be,

I am drawing in

frantically I wait for it all to end.

TO COVID-19

In these times of social distancing,
Distancing myself from my usual self
Selfishly withdrawing from everything.

Everything is all upside down
Down to family relations,
Relationships I thought would never
Ever change this way.

Weighing on my mind and in my shoulders
Shouldering the stress of these times,
(Time itself seems both endless and frantic)

Jim Carillon

During This Storm

After last night's storm
Fog hugs the valley,
Clouds still heavy above,
The sun strains to appear.

Over and over these days
I find myself retreating to
Paul Simon's "Kathy's Song",
Striving to relive a simpler time.

A time long before the current crisis,
Even before the regular strains of
Contemporary life prior to this madness,
When looking forward was once possible.

All my usual tricks are useless now.
Social distance is killing me slowly,
My reason for being challenged again,
"Writing songs I can't believe."

I have learned life goes on without me,
The air itself now clearer for some.
Poet friends expressing this crisis better,
Making good use of this forced pause.

Yet for me the storm continues,
Finding no shelter from wind or rain—
"I stand alone without beliefs,"
Without hope for the sun again.

Corona Days

Out of sorts
Out of breath
Out of touch
Out of my mind

Too much bad news
Too much tv news
Too much worry
Too much food

Not enough sports
Not enough to go around
Not enough compassion
Not enough loving

Testing gaps
Wash your hands
Social distancing
Avoid all gatherings

Many uncertainties remain:
Where will it strike next?
Who will it strike next?
When will this nightmare be over?

IDENTITY

In the middle of my sleep last night I had the first stanza
Of my next poem well framed in my head—repeating it as I turned over.
But this morning all of it—including the theme—has completely vanished.
Maybe this will finally teach me to put a pad on the nightstand.

Yet I suspect there is something larger going on here:
Of late my dreams seem so intense yet fleeting when I awake.
My subconscious clearly is working on something vital
But what can it be; what is so damn important?

My current life seems relatively calm,
Especially when I think of earlier times of more intense stress.
Maybe that's the problem—not enough personal strain these days?
Am I not strong without the immediate challenge to be so?

Or more likely and thankfully it is not all about me:
So many others are suffering intensely in these troubled times.
There is so much need for genuine service to others—
To which of these many opportunities should I commit?

Ahh, now I think I see what the problem is—
What my recurring vulnerability is yet again.
No wonder my sleep has recently become so fitful.
Who am I really and how shall I next serve?

Fynnley!

Expecting Again after So Many Years

Today my wife and I checked off yet another step
On an extensive journey of preparations
For us to soon become approved foster parents
For an as-yet-unknown child in need.

Months of countless classes and obligations:
Physicals, fingerprinting, background checks, home visits,
Extensive surveys of our family background and personal needs—
All necessary but invasive and seemingly endless.

Intense evening classes and homework about what fostering might entail,
Seemingly designed in part to weed out couples or individuals
Not fully prepared for the complicated roles and responsibility
Of temporarily caring for and loving someone else's child.

Frequent warnings of how difficult it will likely be for us and the child,
The importance of co-parenting whenever possible with the birth family,
And the total lack of influence the foster family will have on
The ultimate placement of a child after the unknowable duration of our foster care.

How do we come to love this child in such desperate need—
Shelter her, nurture him, feed and clean her, teach him,
And provide all the love and emotional support we can muster
Only to help this child someday return to an uncertain future?

Then again, with all our resources and love we have to offer,
How can we NOT do this for some child in need?

FOSTERING

Hopes and expectations dashed, or are they?
Our first foster infant promised four days ago—
A perfect fit for him and us.

Case worker: "Plan to spend tomorrow at the hospital
Learning to care for him given his premature issues,
Then likely take him home tomorrow night."

We share this great news with our family,
Light a candle at church for our new son.
Can't wait for the morning call to meet him!

No call the next day, and the next,
And the next.
Only the case worker can call—she hasn't.

She calls tonight: "Still searching for a family member
To care for him while birth mother is in jail.
You might not be the family caring for him after all."

Is our life, our breath, on hold a few days more?
What really is best for him?
Don't know whether to hope now or not.

And how do we grieve for a foster child we have not met?

WELCOME HOME FYNNLEY!

You're ours!
Or rather we are yours for a while.
After hopes dashed with fears that
Someone else might care for you,
We bring you home today!

Days at the hospital learning how to care
For a newborn and each other.
Changing you, feeding you, holding you
Has fully grabbed our hearts.

Welcome home Mr. Fynnley
To your nursery, your crib, your foster family
Who already loves you sooooo.
Much fun awaits
Along with trying times soon enough.

What an adventure we all shall have!

1:00 A.M. FEEDING
(WITH DIVERTICULITIS)

The pain came roaring back tonight
After telling the doctor this afternoon
That all was finally well.
Silly me.

Wishing for it to be true
I again jumped the gun:
Doing what I shouldn't have
Too soon.

The stakes are much higher now
Taking on this big challenge,
Yet slapped down by sickness
Once again.

At times my body brings me up short
Despite my good intentions.
My new infant son needs me to
Get better.

And oh, how I already need him too.

WORRIES AND THEIR ANTIDOTES

Pervasive climate change with too few taking personal responsibility for reversing it;
Feeding a bottle to our infant son.
Severe income and wealth disparities with institutional forces only growing the gap;
Shouldering him for heart to heart time.

Continuing racial and economic injustices further encouraged by the powerful;
Sharing our new foster son with our community.
Health care and the necessary insurance to support it denied to those needing it most;
Watching him sleep in his crib.

Narcissistic political leaders and the many people who helped to put them in charge;
Rocking gently until he falls asleep.
Violence, wars and greed through our entire world;
Watching my wife sing to and nuzzle our son.

When we accepted the life-altering challenges of foster parenting,
My wife and I were striving for social justice, trying to help other families in need.
I now realize that by loving this child so completely,
We ease the intractable worries in our lives.

Getting Ready

Make more formula
Change and feed the baby
Every three hours
Momma's coming home.

Stroll him three miles
Trim the front hedges
Launder our clothes
Mamma's coming home.

Give him a bath
Cuddle till he sleeps
Try to take your nap
Mamma's coming home.

Sweep the floors
Finish the leftovers
Shower and shave
Mamma's coming home tonight!

Sleeping Together

There's a reason why young people have babies:
It's exhausting for those of us in our late sixties.
The buzz from the lack of sleep makes it harder
Still there are moments that make it all worthwhile.

We are advised to sleep when he sleeps
However short these naps are.
They do help for a while yet I long
For six straight hours of deep sleep.

One solution sometimes works wonders:
As he snuggles against my chest
Getting ready to sleep himself,
I just lay back on my bed, the two of us together.

It doesn't last for long (too bad),
But it is so comforting for us both.
Heart to heart and four eyes closed.
Nothing better in the world!

Balancing Act

Where is the right balance . . .

between the fog from my lack of sleep
and intense mutual connections with our infant?

between the unrelenting demands of his care
and the many comforts we provide each other?

between admiration of my wife's mothering love
and the intimacy we now too rarely share?

between the undeniable good we are doing for our community
and required narrowing of our connections with this community?

between the life-changing, rewarding journey of foster parenting
and our individual growth and emotional well-being?

Desperately searching for balance
and at this moment wondering if it is achievable.

Dear Mommy (3 Months old in just 3 days!)

September 13, 2019

Thank you for your beautiful letter. I hope to see you again soon too.

My foster parents (Grammie and Poppie) are taking quite good care of me. I love being held by them and playing with them. Poppie takes me for an hour stroller ride almost every morning. Grammie plays with me on a floor gym where I swing my arms and legs at hanging soft creatures that move when I swat them. She and Poppie turn me over for some belly time where I scooch some but haven't learned to crawl yet. I can turn over sometimes from my belly to my back—exciting for all of us! Grammie and I share music together and I love it when she sings to me. They both also read me books but I'm not too interested in these just yet.

I am learning to smile at Grammie and Poppie who really seem to like it when I do. We do love each other so much. I guess it is the least I can do for them taking such good care of me. I don't use words yet (it will be a long time before that) but I'm pretty good at making my needs known. Poppie and Grammie seem to know exactly what I need. The food is good and plentiful, and I continue to gain weight (eating is what I do very well.)

I meet lots of loving people who Grammie and Poppie seem to know. There is a growing community of people who enjoy visiting with me. I go to church with my foster parents, to a community garden where I help grow vegetables for people in need, was a big hit at Poppie's poetry group recently and even visited a college this past week. (Just keeping my options open for the future.) I have met lots of helpful doctors too. So glad now to be rid of that silly oxygen tank.

I have my very own room with a comfortable crib. A babbling brook plays when they put me down to sleep. I like being swaddled when I sleep so my busy arms and legs don't wake me up too soon. The best though is my changing table right next to a window. When Grammie or Poppie changes my diaper, I like to look out at the trees just outside my window. I enjoy the trees on my stroller rides too, although it is so peaceful that I often fall asleep during these rides.

Thanks for the picture you drew with your letter. As you can probably tell from above, I'm pretty much a prince in Poppie and Grammie's house too.

I hope your time-out is short and I get to see you again real soon,

Much love, Fynnley

PS: Here are two pictures from this morning's stroll: One is at a neighborhood playground where I am dreaming about playing with Poppie on this equipment someday soon. The other picture is me next to Grammie's lovely flowerpot. Isn't this the most beautiful thing you ever saw? The flowers look pretty nice too.

Foster Parenting

Go my little turtle, go
Down this sandy beach
From your warm nest
To the crashing sea.

I will stand guard
Against unseen predators,
Protect you as you crawl
This first difficult path.

Once in the waves
I can no longer join you,
Save you from other dangers
That still lie ahead.

But I can give you a
Good start and safe passage
During this crucial portion of
Your hopefully long journey.

God speed, little one.

New Best Friends

Sitting here with you on my lap
Makes it harder than usual to draft this poem
But I can't put you down just yet.

Blowing your bubbles and sucking on my wrist,
You just want to play more with your Poppie.
Believe me, I get it.

Now at four months you are loads of fun too.
All smiles when I pay enough attention to you,
Making it impossible not to do whatever you want.

I have no idea when it will happen,
But someday I must give you up
Long before I am ready.

This, this is the curse of fostering:
Providing a good start in life that you so richly deserve,
Loving you deeply, then reluctantly letting you go.

So, let's play more while we still can
And I'll forget that someday will ever come:
Being here with you now as best friends forever.

At Five Months

Frequent lack of sleep
Catching up with me:
Low brain-buzz all day,
Movements slower, concentration harder.

His sleep schedule works
For him and my wife,
Less well for me.
Need him sleeping through the night soon.

Yet he smiles easily now,
Recognizes and comforts us
When either of us holds him.
Feeding him is special for us all.

As always, a mixed bag:
Challenges and rewards,
Doing what we can for others,
Reaping unexpected benefits.

I just hope we develop
An even deeper bond
That meets all our needs
Before we part too soon.

Domesticated

Infant changed then strolled three miles to the park and back,
Played on the floor awhile then read two cardboard books.
Sang his customized "Twinkle, Twinkle …" sleepy song
As I gently laid him down for his morning nap.

Flannel sheets smoothed and fitted corners tightly tucked—
Hospital-corners on the bottom didn't need it this time.
Duvet bedspread taught enough to bounce a dime,
Throw pillows placed exactly where she insists they must be.

Breakfast dishes washed then placed in the dishwasher—
I know, seems redundant doesn't it?
Kitchen counters wiped (with separate sponge)
And bib and wipe cloths thrown into laundry.

Washed and shammy'd both cars last evening before
It got too dark to see the streaks. Garaged them then
Checked tires and filled the washer reservoirs.
After dinner laundered two loads while watching tv news.

Just now checked and responded to emails and
Updated accounting from online bank statement.
Put away papers from yesterday's meetings and
Slightly revised my last poem once again.

Just a lazy Saturday morning in retirement.

Early Christmas Gift

Aline and I received our Christmas gift early
this year way before December 25th.
Our foster son arrived June 16th and we brought him
home from the hospital shortly thereafter.

He has blessed us every day since
with many special moments to share:
feeding him brings each of us great joy,
even changing a messy diaper makes us all happier.

Fun times include daily walks
with him in his stroller to the park and back,
hiking with him on my back Tuesday mornings,
or just rolling around on the floor together.

Cuddling when reading books before bedtime,
so many smiles and making silly sounds of all sorts.
Sharing a special nap just this morning in the big bed,
or kisses on both cheeks just for fun.

Photos of special moments with family and friends,
receiving support from other foster families and staff,
even traveling with him snuggly in his rear seat bucket
makes every journey all the more special.

The joys of sharing him with our loving communities:
letting others love on him and hold him,
so many people stepping up to help us,
amazed at our journey at this time of life.

You see, we thought we could help others
with some of the love we had to give.
What we didn't realize is how this love
would be returned to us ten-fold.

So, thank you Fynnley and all of you
who helped all three of us in so many ways,
making this special time with him
the best Christmas gift ever.

MERRY CHRISTMAS to all of you!

Jim Carillon

REASON #847 FOR FOSTERING OUR INFANT SON

Darkened societal skies
More clouds and rain
Uncertain conditions
Ad infinitum

Surgeries cancelled
Touching eliminated
Huge economic losses
Productive work gone

Vague promises
With leaders lying
Infection and death
Tolls rapidly climbing

                        Yet you smile easily
                        Sleep comfortably
                        Share your enthusiasm
                        Continue to grow

                        As long as we protect you
                        No virus will contain you
                        Your joy and human cries
                        Do more than sustain us

                        Thank you for arriving
                        Just in time to
                        Give us hope that
                        These times too shall pass

Happy First Birthday

When you first entered our lives
We couldn't believe our good fortune.
Such a sweet little baby even if
We didn't get much sleep at first.

But now you are even better as you've
Grown into quite a beautiful little boy.
Now trying to keep up with your greater movements,
Your smiles and frequent laughter light our days.

Strolling with you each morning is good for us both
And you have become quite a good hiker on my back.
Reading stories and singing songs with Grammie
Is special to watch and admire in you both.

So many people in our greater community
Have fallen deeply in love with you too.
No wonder as you so enjoy each social event
Sharing widely the joy you bring to us all.

So today on your first birthday
Know that we thank you for who you are,
For all the good times you have brought us, and
Our love always follows you wherever you go.

Poppie and Grammie, June 2020

Morning Strolls with Our Foster Son

Today a longer walk than usual for us
Down the ridge to the community park and beyond.
He turns thirteen months this very day,
Seemingly enjoying our daily hikes or strolls.

Briskly we circle the track at the park
At a pace for this flat mile that is exactly
Twice as slow as my earlier 10K running pace
But speed no longer matters at my age or his.

Onward we roll through neighborhood hills
Looking in separate meadows for a few
Horses to provide a bite of carrot for each,
Yet sadly none were there this cloudy morn.

Instead rubber ducky entertains a while then
Later a plucked Queen Anne's Lace flower.
He begins his morning nap as we climb the ridge home
Despite my attempts to engage him awake.

I treasure these daily walks
Probably even more than he does
And wonder what if anything
He will ever remember of them.

To Our Son

The end of our time together soon approaches.
We always knew this time must come someday
But knowing and feeling are two different things.
I will miss you hopefully more than you'll ever know.

Our role was to provide you a good start,
To launch you successfully on your way.
While we have done this and perhaps a little more,
How will we fill the hole you now leave behind?

I personally thought we were doing it all for you,
Giving back to community in such a personal way.
What I didn't realize was how much you would give us,
How completely you would change our lives for the better.

We have struggled as all persons in relationships do,
Learning how to communicate, how best to love each other.
And we have shared much in this wondrous journey—
Moments and memories I shall always treasure.

As you are now ready to take this next step
Know we are always with you in spirit if no longer in person.
May your future be as bright as the love you have shared
And thank you for all you have done for me and for us.

Love always,
your foster Poppie

Jim Carillon

Foster Leaving Time

We knew this day was coming—
The day we finally pay the piper.
Yet the horror of anyone receiving our child
Outweighs all rational considerations.

In many ways we have long prepared for this,
Doing all we can for him before this day.
"Look at the good start you gave him,"
Our kind friends say. Yet our pain remains.

He has simply changed our lives completely,
Filling an empty bucket I didn't know we had.
Our cup more than run over with all he gave us,
He just growing and being himself.

We remind ourselves how much better it will be
For him moving on to a younger loving family—
All along we have so wanted just this for him.
But the pain of him leaving now creates a huge hole for us.

Be brave my son as you go.
Maybe remember hiking on my back in the woods,
The custom song each time we laid you to sleep,
The fun of the chase, or perhaps swinging at the park.

We won't ever forget these times
Or how special you will always be to us.

LOVED AND LOST AGAIN

Sometimes you simply endure the pain.
Friends search for a silver lining
And share it to try to comfort me
Or perhaps to assure themselves.

But the pain always remains mine.
Grace in the face of it is the goal but
Anger and judgement make that difficult
If not impossible in the short run.

Intellectually this loss was predictable
But that doesn't reduce the emotion,
The feelings of loss and being lost in it.
I must deal with the pain myself.

So I buck up and carry on,
Dwell in it if I must for a while,
To feel the full brunt of the pain
Then much later move on.

What else is there to do?

Quiet Morning Stroll

We emerge from the fog along Cane Creek
To find we have the park all to ourselves.
The quiet broken only by a few commuters
Heading west early to their jobs in the city.

Our stroll to the park so early we
Used the blinking lamp only once
So the oncoming driver could see us
As we borrow a little of his lane.

The sun low behind the eastern hills
Turns the sky a soft butter yellow.
As I lift you to the swing you smile, pointing
To the three-quarters moon in the western sky.

We circle the path around the park and a crow
Greets our arrival high in a silver buckeye tree
That long ago dropped its nuts, its brown leaves
Crackling softly underfoot next to the creek.

The creek barely audible after the last few days
Of sunshine have lowered its constant flow.
Two bluebirds light on another tree branch,
Curious about us early intruders I suspect.

With the sky slowly brightening we hear a dog bark
And more birds serenade us as we walk home,
A chickadee clearly calling among these songs.
Drivers now wave with more of them going around us.

It's 50 degrees or so—cool enough for your sweatshirt
And shoes but not so cold for socks on your hands.
You kick off your lap blanket a couple of times
Before we climb the final drive to our ridge.

Soon you will be leaving us as it's now time
For your transition to a permanent family.
I will miss these early morning strolls with you,
Especially quieter walks when the world is entirely ours.

Missing You Already

It is the small daily rituals that we already miss the most:
Lifting you out of your crib and hugging you closely for a few extra seconds.
Changing your diaper and clothes in front of your window so you can see the trees.
Ending your bath each night with your joyous splashing to get me wet too.

Chasing you across our big bed for tickles and giggles.
Reading picture books in the rocking chair and repeating the fun snoring page.
Feeding you in your highchair with your preferred food from my dinner plate.
Sneaking a peak while you are napping flat out in your crib.

Chasing you as you crawl so fast across the room and sweeping you up for a big kiss.
Playing peek-a-boo and you hiding under the blanket from us too.
Strolling you to the park each morning and pushing you on the swings.
You asking for more as we feed you, on the swings, in your bath and for more kisses.

You pointing to "Alexa" to play some favorite recorded songs from long ago
While rocking you and singing the romantic lyrics softly to you.
Later singing your go-to-sleep song with special lyrics written just for you
And you grabbing Paddy Bear as your essential sleeping companion.

We always wanted you to move from our foster care
To another loving family who will keep you and love you forever.
Now that you so gracefully made this transition just this week,
Know that we already miss you and will always love you too.

Writing

This Virgin Page

This virgin page stares at me
So full of promise, potential unrealized,
Like this morning's cold bright winter sky
Intimidating in her stark glare.

How can I bring her potential to fruition
Without spoiling or damaging her beyond repair?
Add meaning without cluttered confusion;
Share feelings without demanding expectations?

Maybe I should just let her be,
Wait, observe more, get a better grip,
Before intervening to who knows what end.
Listen rather than solve what isn't a problem.

But she stares back so expectantly
Wanting me to do something, anything
Until I think I might. Then I begin to doubt again
Whether any move, any word, could help or only hurt.

I walk away wondering
If on another day I might do more,
Do something meaningful
Just for her.

Sweet Nectarine

Smooth scarlet skin protects your bright yellow flesh
Which shelters a blood red pit in your very center.
You nourish my nose and my eyes,
Later my very core as well.

A tiny speck lodges between two front teeth
As I vainly struggle to free it from this gap,
Telling myself that it surely will dislodge itself
Joining the rest sliding slowly down within me.

The warmth of your colors portends another glow
As my body converts flesh into sugar then
Sugar into energy for movement or thought—
Either way you will have warmed me twice.

Like Henry chopping wood for his fireplace
On the edge of a distant pond—warmed twice.
I pray that someday I will be this useful, this luscious,
When giving my own warmth and beauty to

Someone somewhere who might appreciate this gift.

My Charge

On our zodiac boat ride late this afternoon,
The furthest distance from our western starting point,
Past all five of the quaint Cinque Terra villages,
Was Porto Venere on the edge of the Gulf of Poetica.

How fitting I thought this distant bay was
For someone such as this struggling poet
During this journey so far from home,
Wondering what I might next capture and describe.

We turned about at this distant spot—
Reorienting our craft, pointing it toward the setting sun,
Back to the start of our seaward journey—
That is, returning from whence we came.

Isn't this exactly my charge for this poet's current life journey?

After All

Like half a chocolate birthday cake
Under tax prep papers which
Tomorrow I must remember
To take to friends at church.

Like a noisy baby eating
Pureed peas in his highchair
After half his bottle of formula
Which is all he really wants.

Like the dense fog earlier that
Shrouded our morning stroller walk
To the park but not quite hiding
Three bucket loads of litter retrieved.

Like this unusually warmer winter,
Much cloudier than last year so that
Our solar panels produce less power,
But less is needed with this warmer weather.

Like these minor contradictions,
I can't decide what to write
But vainly attempt to write something
To make some sense of all this.

Maybe there is a poem here after all.

TOO MANY WORDS
~~(13th revision)~~

too many words ~~some~~ / yet more
cut by half then cut ~~some~~ / more
less context, less writing
more editing: show don't tell

fewer memories more *now*
less grammar no punctuation
twist the end but no summary
less rock more roll

more clarity, more ambiguity
~~and way more~~ clever/er (is that a word?)
more universal less personal
but don't take this personally

less description more detail
less prose more poetry
more for the reader less about you
period.

now go back and do it again

Managing Stress

My organizing skills have served me well
In times of great stress and uncertainty,
Planning or at least anticipating well
Challenges that undoubtably face us all.

Yet my right-brain rational thinking,
This calendaring of my life only takes me so far;
More likely it gets in the way of me
Knowing and dealing with important moments.

Oh, to become the true artist, musician or perhaps poet
Who reaches deeply within
To vividly produce a unique view of the world
Then reaches out to connect this vision to all.

This is who I now strive to become.

Some Days Are Like That

Another day wasted
Without a specific event
Planned on my busy calendar,
This day just slips away.

Eating too much with
TV news blaring on and on,
Checking emails endlessly,
Losing often at internet hearts.

Exercising neither my body nor mind
Waiting for inspiration to strike.
But she remains elusive as ever,
Visiting someone else I assume.

Petty concerns of one too comfortable.
Life neither tragic nor dramatic enough
To write something meaningful or worthy,
Or even modestly helpful.

Maybe tomorrow will be better
When I'm busier or more thoughtful,
More engaged with the world,
Less focused on me.

Dear Aja Monet

I am with you.
The big crimes keep coming,
Pushing down those
Who work the hardest
And get the least.

No wonder they
Call it Capitalism;
Those with the capital
Continue to take
From those without.

This is why I do
What I due,
Why we all must
Do what we due,
Straining to bend the arc.

To reverse this madness
It will take all of us
Not only showing the pain
But doing something about it.
Help us fight the good fight against
The attitude of what's in it for me.

ONLY TEN LINES?

The assignment: write a poem about writing a poem in ten lines
or less.

Are you kidding? I'm lucky if I can cut my poems down to one
page!
That's like sleeping through the night without getting up once,
Or even just sleeping through the night.

Do you realize it's always easier to upshift level than downshift
up a steep hill?
Maybe I'll use long lines.
But then again who wants to listen to an old geezer anyways?

What comes to mind is the last line of a song from Pink Floyd:
"Thought I'd something more to say..."
Cue the electric guitar strumming a single seventh chord.

This White Page

This blank white page screams at me:
Add something meaningful or at least important!
Add color and depth with some printed words!
Yet today nothing of substance flows forth.

Sometimes my perspective is just too narrow,
My own experience and wisdom frankly pale
Compared to the many better writers
Who speak so eloquently with more to say.

I confess my life has been too soft, too easy,
Haven't earned the blues by a long shot.
An unworthy victim of my own many privileges
Despite or because of my efforts to always achieve more.

My early years of struggle have indeed provided
Economic comfort and security for the years ahead.
But at what cost? What have I given up along this route?
More importantly, who else has paid this price for me?

My altruistic efforts now, all my social justice volunteering,
Can't possibly repay these untold costs along the way
No matter how hard I might try. And yet,
What else can I do but begin to make amends?

How about I ask what your concerns are. Listen more deeply.
Show I genuinely care. Build a broader caring community.
Appreciate the beauty you and others bring to this world.
Be open to your wisdom and the strengths of others.

In short, let you influence me, change me,
To be your partner along this journey we both share.
Be the follower of your leadership and your designs,
And truly serve what is best for you and all the others.

Then maybe I'll have something to share on this white page.

Jim Carillon

About the Author

It has been more than three decades since Jim Carillon wooed his wife with romantic songs he wrote for her—though Aline was and remains the finer musician. When he failed his third retirement, he started taking poetry classes at Osher Lifelong Learning Institute (OLLI) at UNC Asheville, where he began to write personal poems instead of songs. He joined the established OLLI Poetry Lover's group, facilitates a second such group there, and meets with a smaller group of writers at his church. Mutually sharing their writing brings some sanity to all of them.

Jim spent years fighting the wars of corporate America as an organizational consultant, trainer, and human resources manager at a greenfield start-up of a team-oriented manufacturing plant. Eventually escaping these challenges, he and Aline created, and for eight years managed, a family-friendly bed-and-breakfast located in a remote corner of the Pisgah National Forest. Then, long after raising two children to fine adults and entering—sort of—full retirement, he and his wife embarked on foster-parenting a newborn—who, as infants invariably do, has completely taken over their lives.

Jim writes of simple day-to-day joys and concerns in between his bicycle commuting, extensive hiking, and volunteering for social justice in the beautiful mountains near Asheville, North Carolina.

Also available from Pisgah Press

Mombie: The Zombie Mom — Barry Burgess
$16.95

Letting Go: Collected Poems 1983-2003 — Donna Lisle Burton
$14.95

Musical Morphine: Transforming Pain One Note at a Time — Robin Russell Gaiser
$17.95

MacTiernan's Bottle — Michael Hopping
$14.95

rhythms on a flaming drum
$16.95

I Like It Here! Adventures in the Wild & Wonderful World of Theatre — C. Robert Jones
$30.00

LANKY TALES
Lanky Tales, Vol. I: The Bird Man & other stories
$9.00
Lanky Tales, Vol. II: Billy Red Wing & other stories
$9.00
Lanky Tales, Vol. III: A Good and Faithful Friend & other stories
$9.00

Red-state, White-guy Blues — Jeff Douglas Messer
$15.95

A Green One for Woody — Patrick O'Sullivan
$15.95

Reed's Homophones: a comprehensive book of sound-alike words — A.D. Reed
$17.95

Swords in their Hands: George Washington and the Newburgh Conspiracy
$24.95 — Dave Richards
Finalist in the USA Book Awards for History, 2014

Trang Sen: A Novel of Vietnam — Sarah-Ann Smith
$19.50

Invasive Procedures: Earthqukes, Calamities, & poems from the midst of life — Nan Socolow
$17.95

THE RICK RYDER MYSTERY SERIES — RF Wilson
Deadly Dancing
$15.95
Killer Weed
$14.95

To order:

Pisgah Press, LLC
PO Box 9663, Asheville, NC 28815
www.pisgahpress.com

www.ingramcontent.com/pod-product-compliance
Lightning Source LLC
Chambersburg PA
CBHW061658040426
42446CB00010B/1799